FIVE 5 FINGER PIANO

3RD EDITION
MOVIE HITS

ISBN 978-1-5400-8901-4

HAL•LEONARD®

Contact us:
Hal Leonard
7777 West Bluemound Road
Milwaukee, WI 53213
Email: info@halleonard.com

In Europe, contact:
Hal Leonard Europe Limited
42 Wigmore Street
Marylebone, London, W1U 2RN
Email: info@halleonardeurope.com

In Australia, contact:
Hal Leonard Australia Pty. Ltd.
4 Lentara Court
Cheltenham, Victoria, 3192 Australia
Email: info@halleonard.com.au

The Ballad of the Lonesome Cowboy
from TOY STORY 4

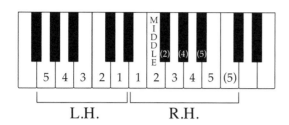

Music and Lyrics by
Randy Newman

Moderately fast

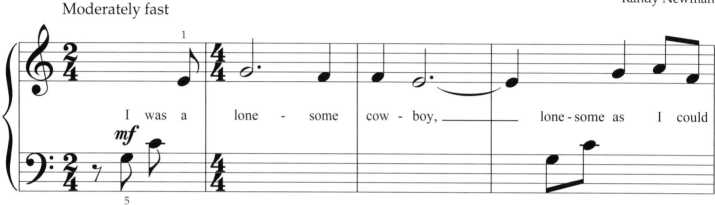

I was a lone - some cow - boy, _____ lone - some as I could

be. You came a - long, changed my life, and fixed what was bro - ken in

Duet Part (Student plays one octave higher than written.)

Moderately fast

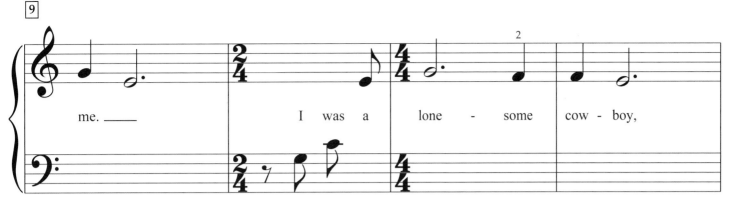

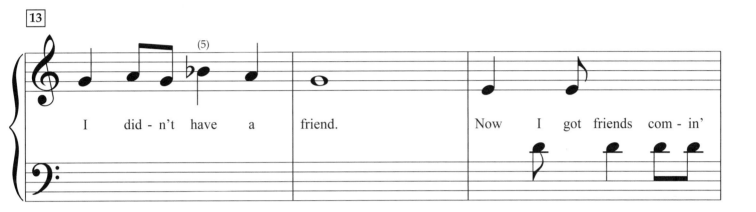

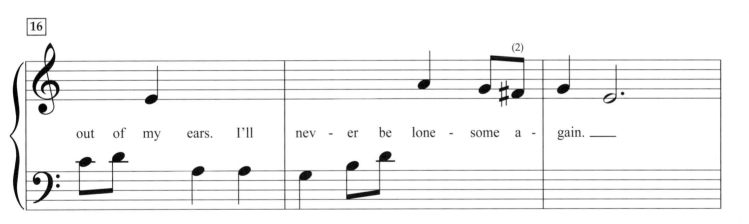

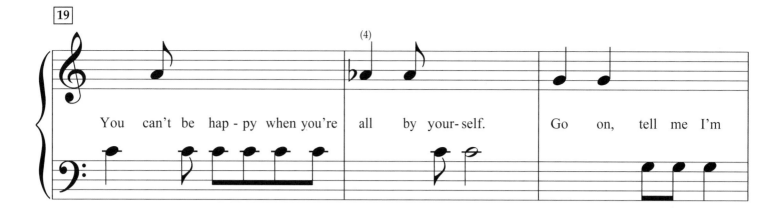

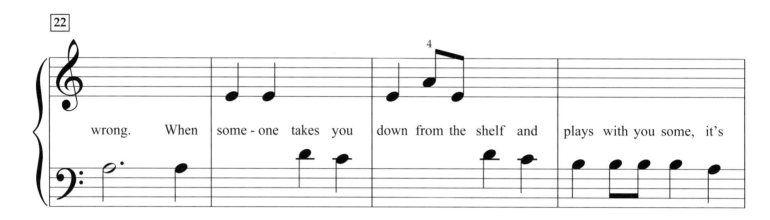

4

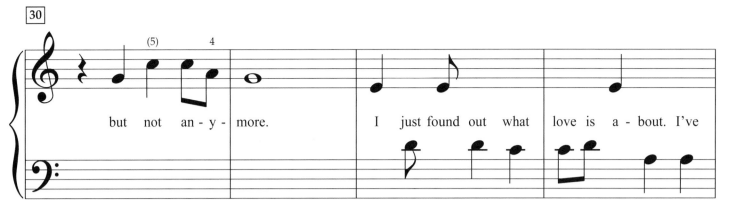

but not an - y - more. I just found out what love is a - bout. I've

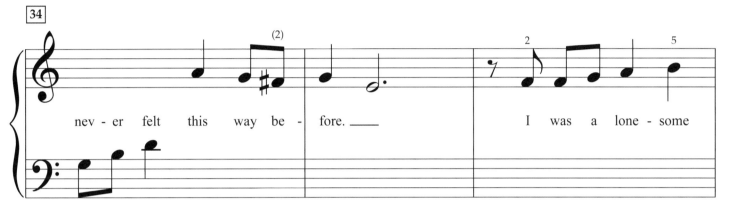

nev - er felt this way be - fore. _____ I was a lone - some

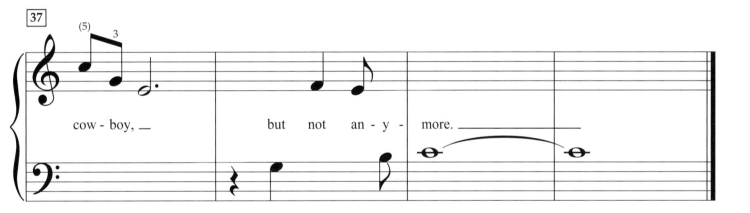

cow - boy, _ but not an - y - more. _____

Downton Abbey
(Theme)

Music by John Lunn

With Motion

Duet Part (Student plays one octave higher than written.)

With motion

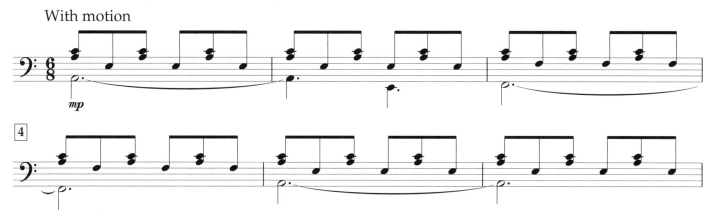

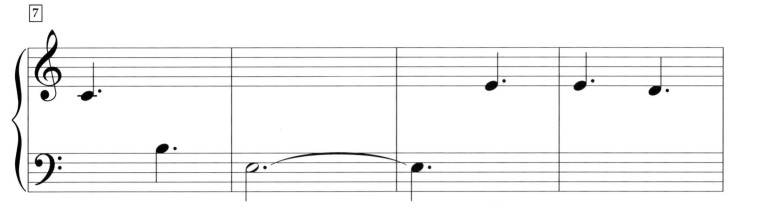

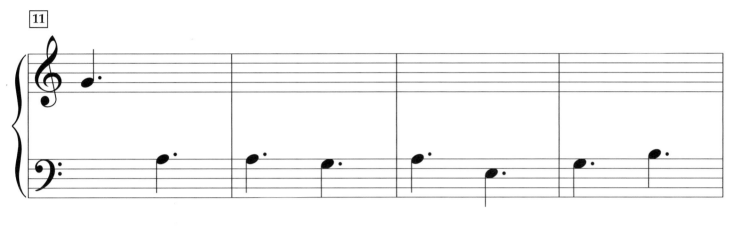

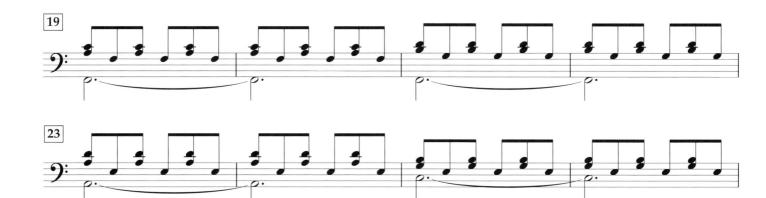

Yesterday
featured in YESTERDAY

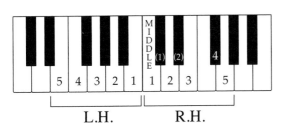

Words and Music by John Lennon
and Paul McCartney

Duet Part (Student plays one octave higher than written.)

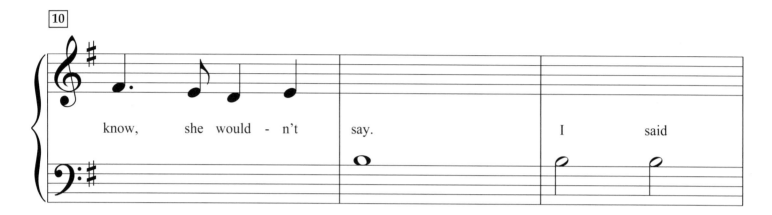

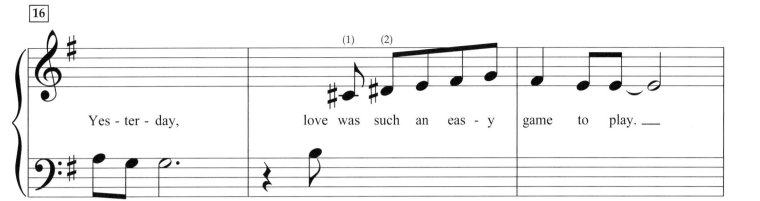

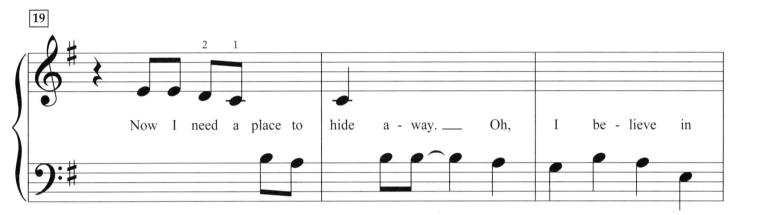

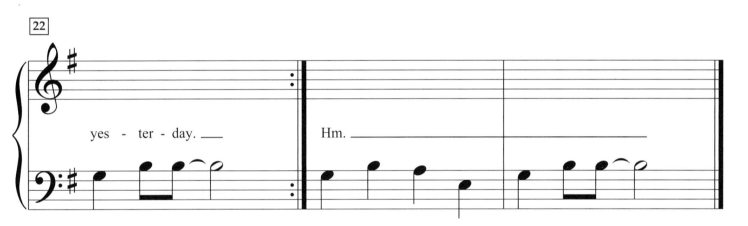

The Place Where Lost Things Go
from MARY POPPINS RETURNS

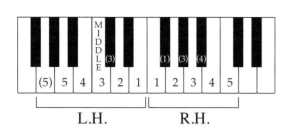

Music by Marc Shaiman
Lyrics by Scott Wittman and Marc Shaiman

Gently, not slow

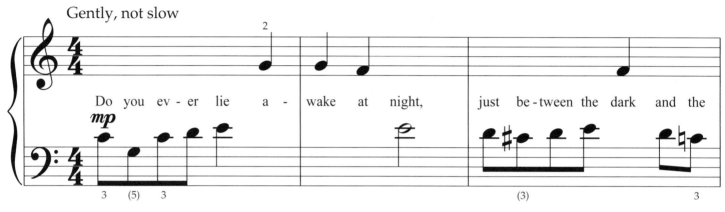

Do you ev - er lie a - wake at night, just be - tween the dark and the

4

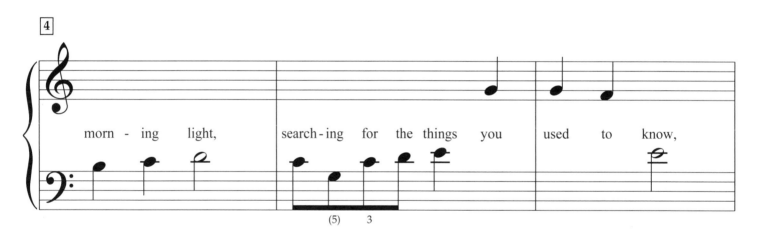

morn - ing light, search - ing for the things you used to know,

Duet Part (Student plays one octave higher than written.)

Gently

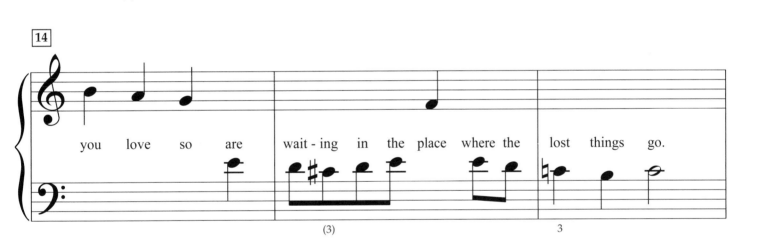

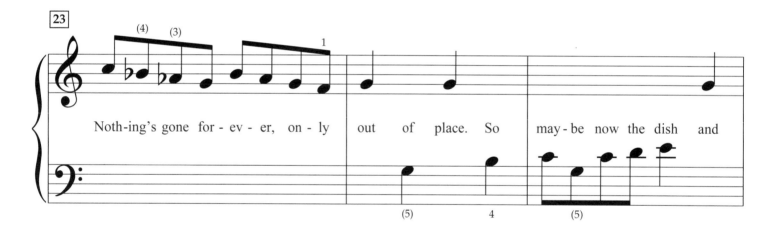

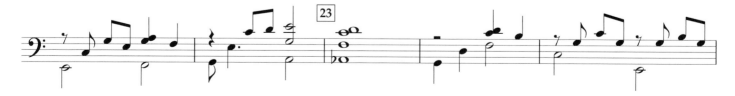

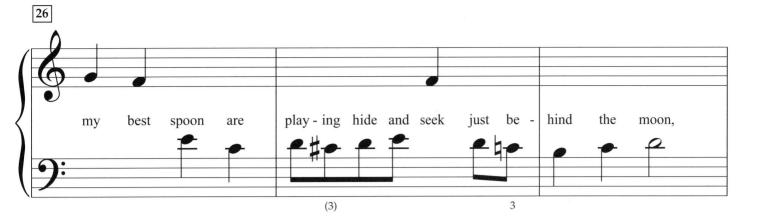

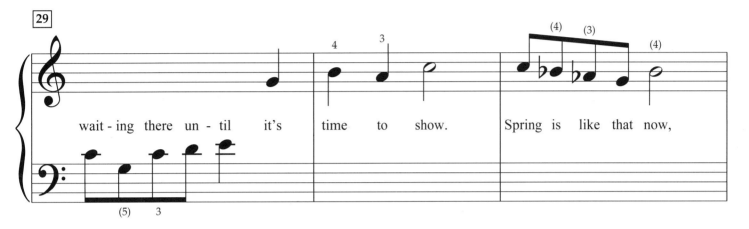

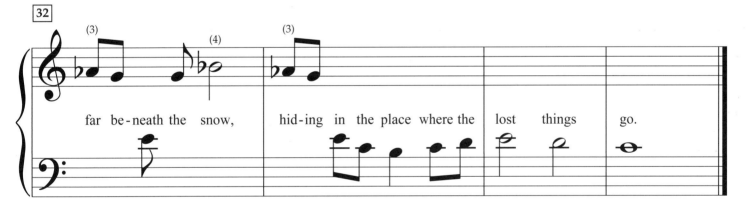

Shallow
from A STAR IS BORN

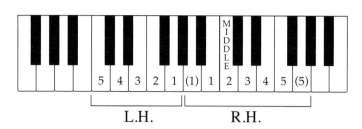

Words and Music by Stefani Germanotta,
Mark Ronson, Andrew Wyatt
and Anthony Rossomando

Moderately

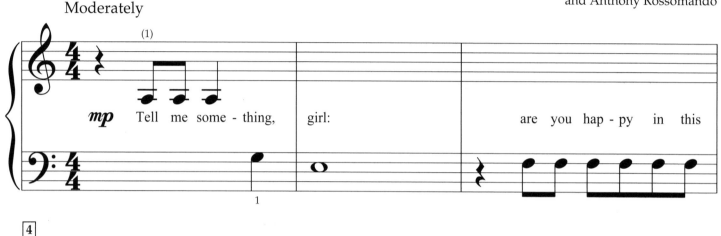

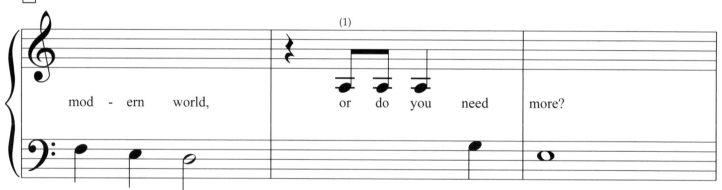

Duet Part (Student plays one octave higher than written.)

Moderately

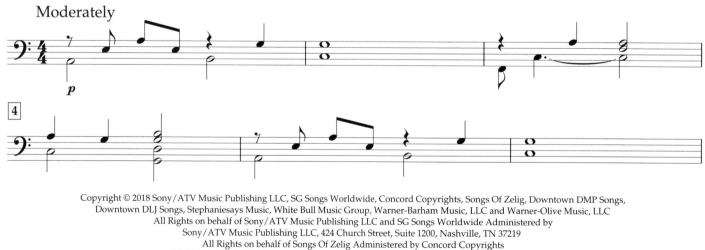

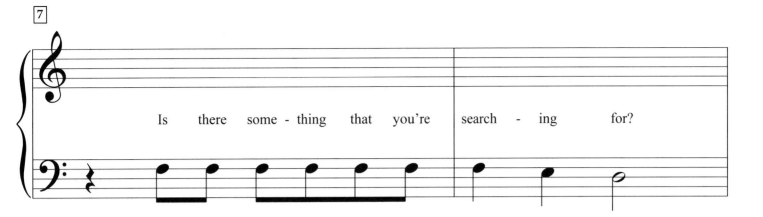

Is there some-thing that you're search - ing for?

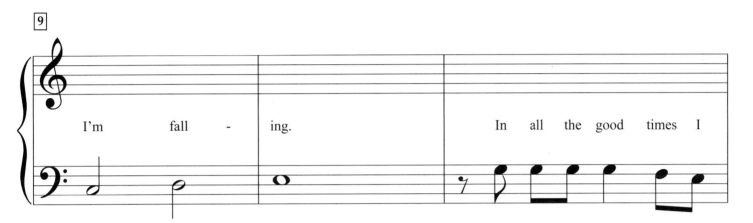

I'm fall - ing. In all the good times I

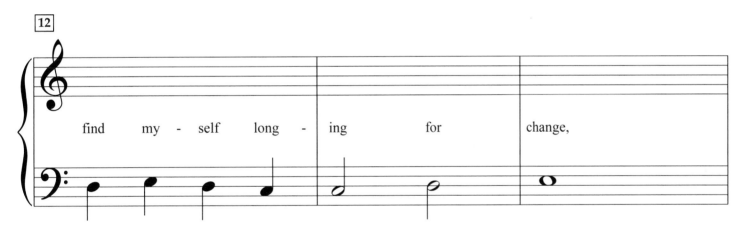

find my - self long - ing for change,

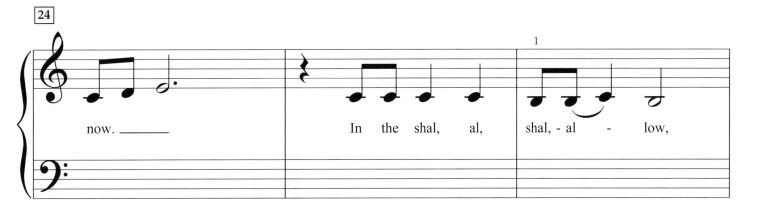

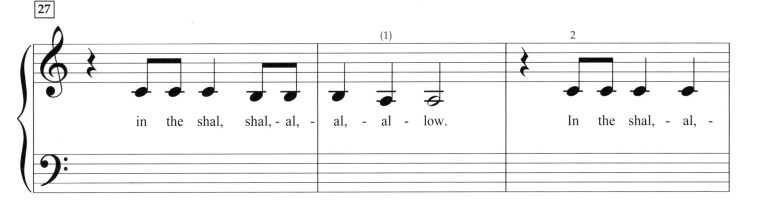

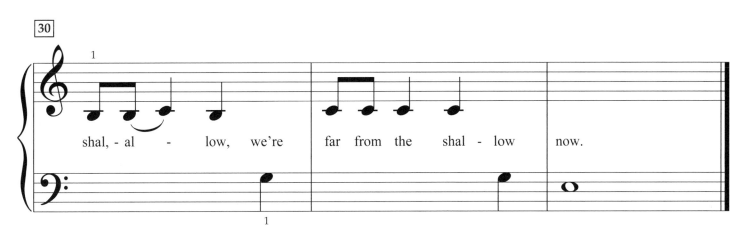

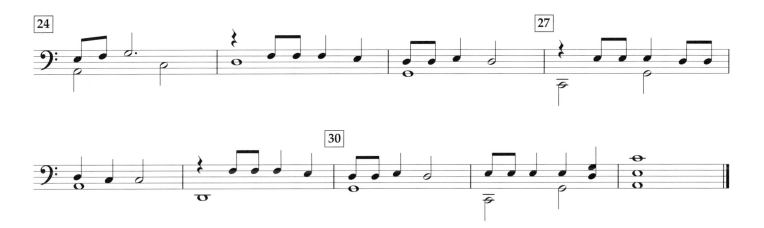

19

Speechless
from ALADDIN

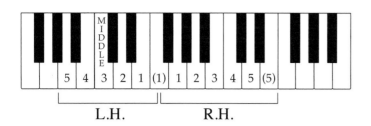

L.H.   R.H.

Music by Alan Menken
Lyrics by Benj Pasek and Justin Paul

Moving along

Here comes a wave meant to wash me a-way, a tide that is tak-ing me un - der. Swal-low-ing sand, left with noth-ing to say, my

Duet Part (Student plays one octave higher than written.)

Moving along

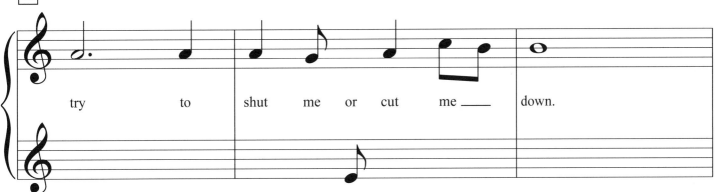

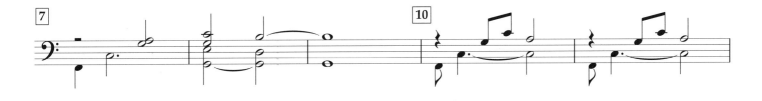

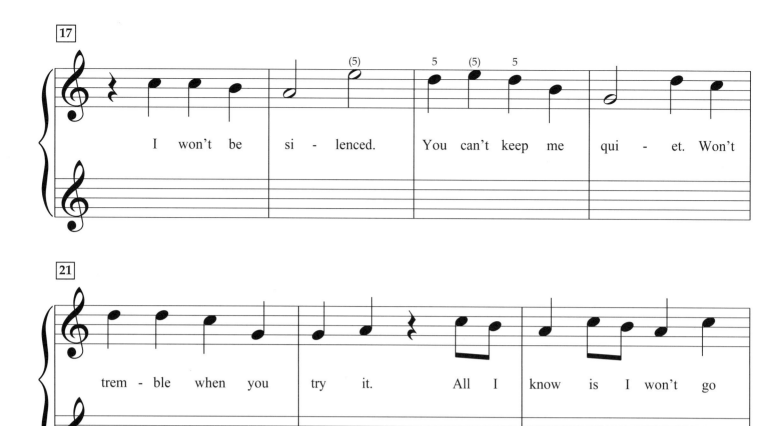

they try to suf - o - cate me. Don't you un - der - es - ti -

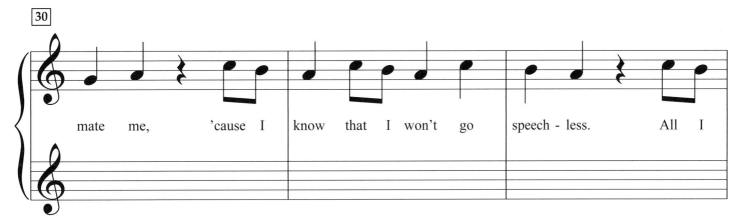

mate me, 'cause I know that I won't go speech - less. All I

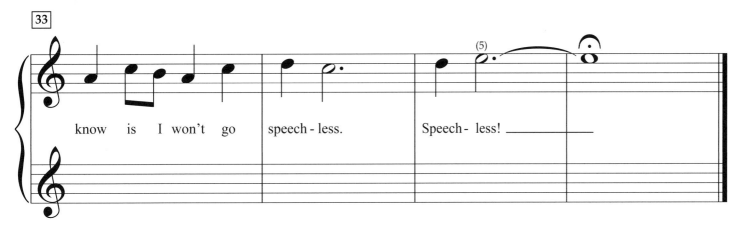

know is I won't go speech - less. Speech - less! _____

Zero
from RALPH BREAKS THE INTERNET

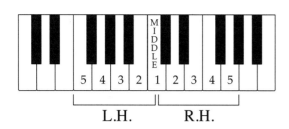

Words and Music by Dan Reynolds,
Wayne Sermon, Ben McKee,
Daniel Platzman and John Hill

With energy

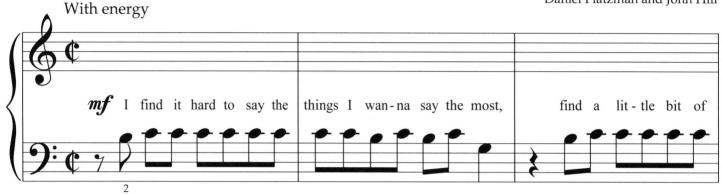

mf I find it hard to say the things I wan-na say the most, find a lit-tle bit of

stead-y as I get close, find a bal-ance in the mid-dle of the cha-os.

Duet Part (Student plays one octave higher than written.)

With energy

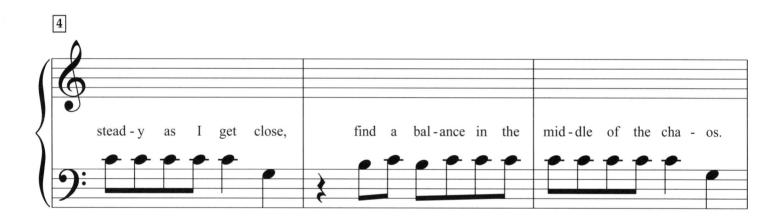

mp

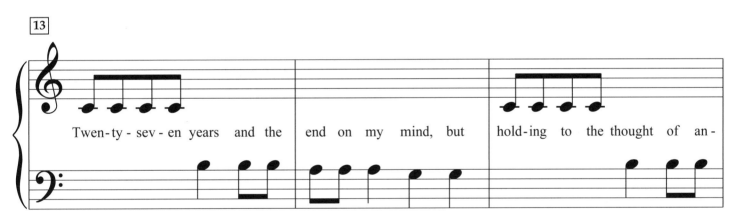

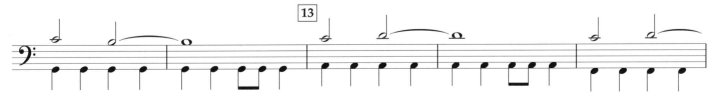

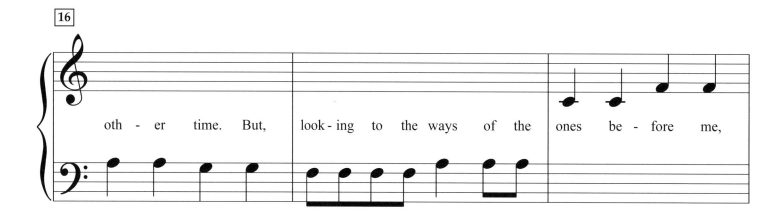

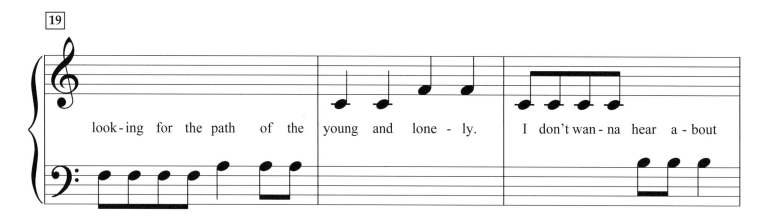

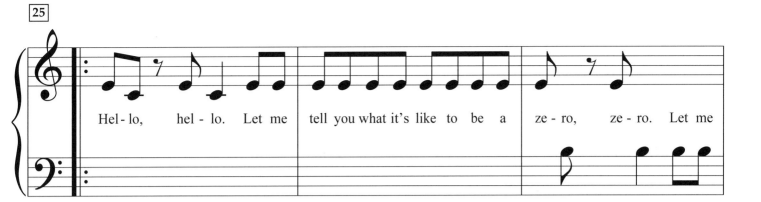

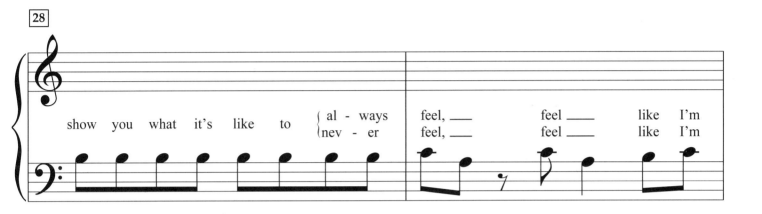

A Million Dreams
from THE GREATEST SHOWMAN

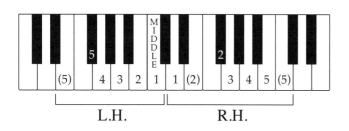

Words and Music by Benj Pasek
and Justin Paul

Moderately, with intensity

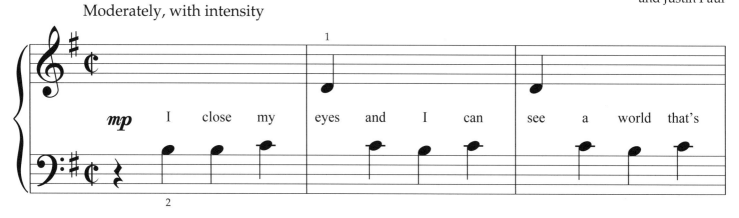

I close my eyes and I can see a world that's

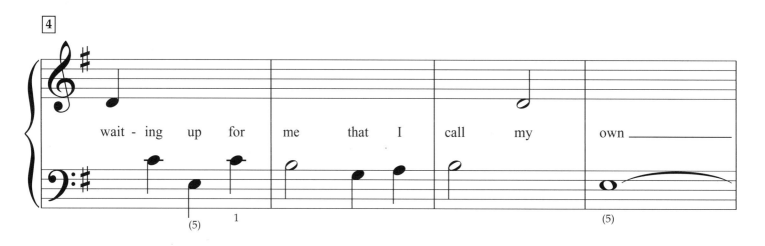

wait - ing up for me that I call my own ____

Duet Part (Student plays one octave higher than written.)

Moderately, with intensity

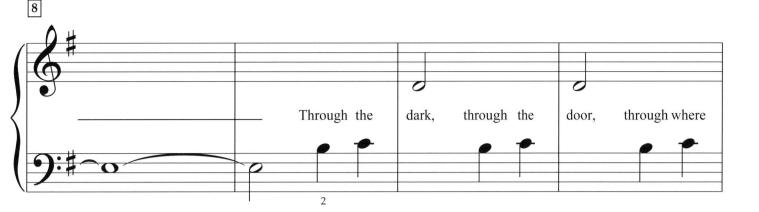

Through the dark, through the door, through where

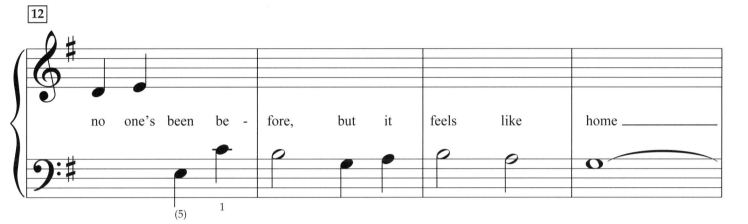

no one's been be - fore, but it feels like home

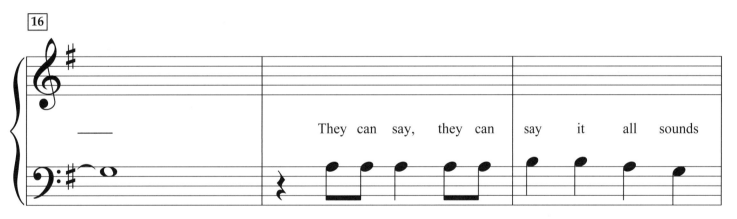

They can say, they can say it all sounds

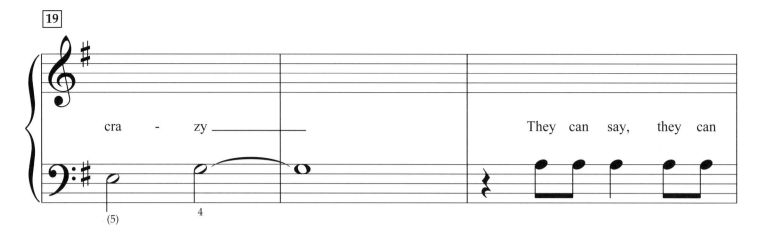

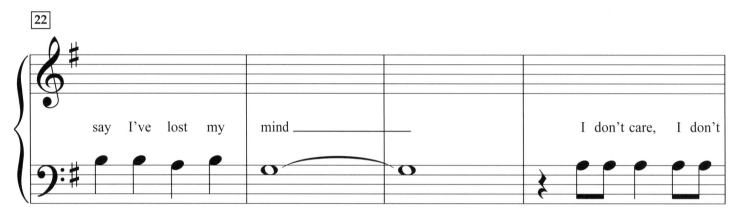

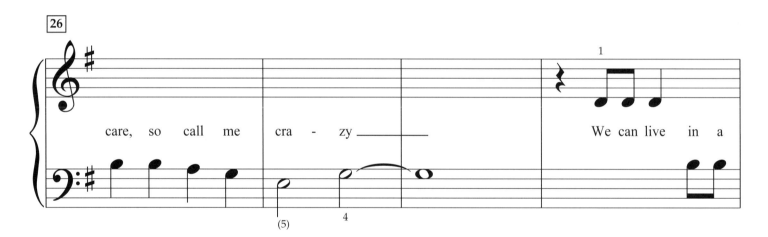

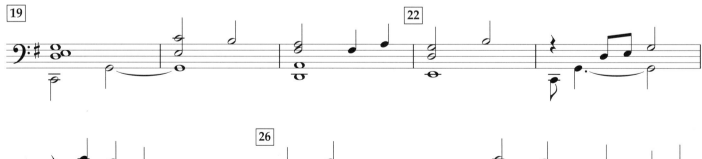

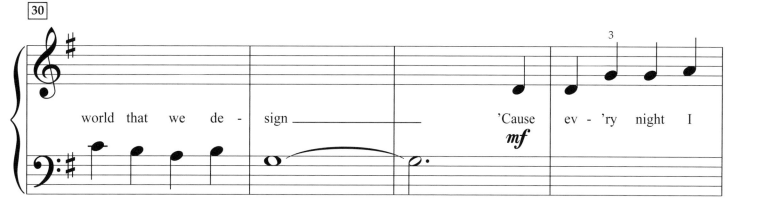

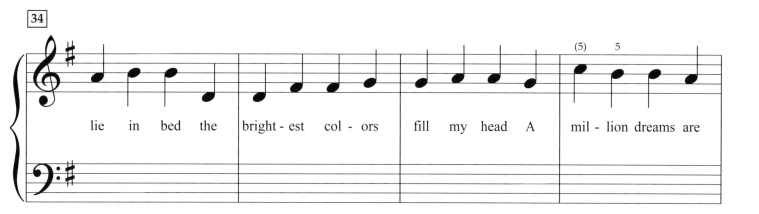

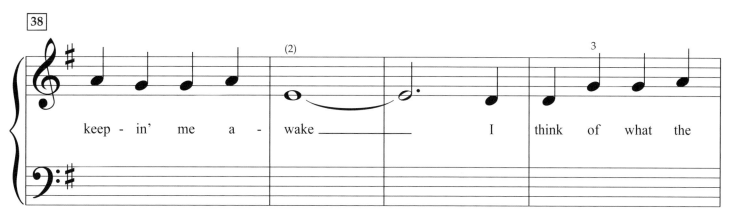

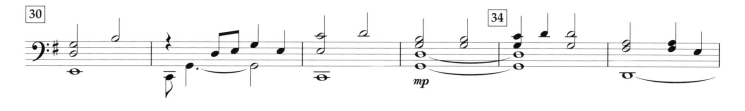

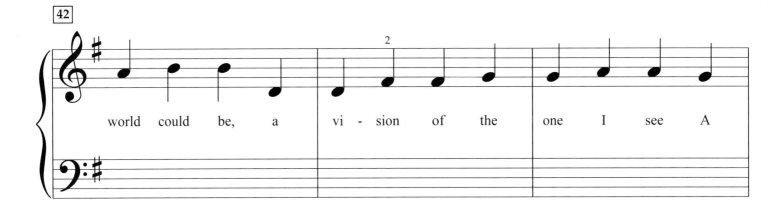

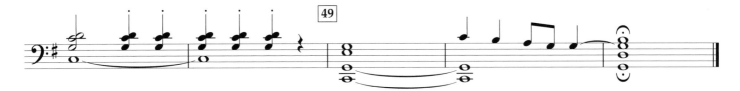